FIERCE

POEMS ABOUT LOVE, TRAUMA AND OTHER WORLDLY THINGS.

SUKRITI SINHA

Made with ♥ on the Notion Press Platform
www.notionpress.com

For Papa

Contents

Contents

Foreword

This book is a collection of what will probably be the closest poems
to my heart.
"all art is art,
and i hope mine is worth something to you. "
Abstract poems will always be the one thing I find the most
solitude in, and I hope my poems make a difference for you as well.

Preface

I have been writing for as long as I can remember. And I don't mean just poems; I mean stories, letters, notes, anything I could possibly get my hands on. It has always been like an addiction, and the biggest comfort.

Writing on my good days helped keep me grounded to the earth, and writing on my bad ones helped remind me of the good days.

I hope reading this book reminds you of your good days as well.

Acknowledgements

I know, for a matter of fact, that I got this gift of words from my father, like every other thing. It makes my heart swell with pride every time I am told I resemble him. That, I think, is the biggest gift of all. I have written this book for every person who has ever supported me, in any and every way, but most of all I have written this book for the only person who would open up a random ice-cream shop for his daughter in the middle of the night just because she said she was craving some. Thank you, Papa, for every little thing you've done for us all. I hope I get to make you juat as proud some day.

I am grateful to my parents, my sister and all my family for never leaving any stone unturned in trying their best to constantly support me.

I am thankful for my teachers for teaching me things that no one else ever could and to my friends for listening to me rant every time a poem did not turn out to be good enough and then staying up with me to make sure I work on it. For making me realise that bad times can give way to great art.

Thank you, my readers, for reading my work and making me feel like my art matters. Thank you for being the reason I have good days at all; thank you for picking this book to read. I hope I don't disappoint.

Prologue

Trigger warning - This book includes poems about abuse, forgotten love, death, suicide, broken friendships and other things one might face trouble with at any point in their lives.

However, it also includes poems about love, care, family, identity, loving oneself, friendships and all things good.

It has taken me a lot of courage to actually publish these. Some, I relate to a bit too much. Others, I don't in the slightest, and hope you never have to either.

Poem

Unsent Letters

1. Unsent Letters -//

if i could go back in time,

i would take you

to the one ice cream store you always loved. you would

describe it

as the one near the apple tree

in the beginning,

because you failed to remember the name.

i liked that about you;

your ability to separate the name

from the characteristics,

and soon, your ability to separate me

from every bad deed i've ever done.

cruel,

how it led you

to separate yourself from me.

a while later,

you used to describe the shop

and i wouldn't have to wait

for you to complete your sentence

- i already knew.

we both knew.

maybe because of the fact

that you love so selflessly,

and foolishly
(both just synonyms, really)
that you used to bring me ice cream
every time i had one of those days,
ones only you could fix,
and hope
that the thing that brought a smile
on your face on your bad days
would do the same for me.
only,
you failed to understand
that ice cream wouldn't matter.
the apple tree wouldn't matter.
all that did matter was you,
time with you
and us.
needless to say,
the ice cream shop
soon became a common favourite.
cruel,
how history is the only thing
we have in common anymore.
i still sign my name
the way you used to like it.
i still order sev barfi
from the same place.
i still think of you when i have donuts.

i still die a little more
every time i remember your laugh.
i still look at paintings
the way you taught me to.
i still write about you.
you will always be my best friend.
i will always write about you.

Abstract

Some Things You Should Know About Me

2. Some Things You Should Know About Me -//

1. i address the harshest lines in my poems to 'you', because i'm not quite sure who i'm most mad at.
2. i might be most mad at myself.
3. my dysfunction tends to be the most intricate part of myself. all that's left of me is shiny and plastic and shallow and i am so tired of hating myself i have almost started liking it that way.
4. i love longing more than i fear love.
5. i am tired of fooling myself. a part of me will always know.
6. i like to think of my scars as signs of escaping the worst.
7. i fear i love my scars so much i do not have the capacity to love anyone else
8. i think hope is the worst.
9. i think my funeral would be empty of people, or even me. my coffin would be filled with paper butterflies stinking with mortality.
10. if i were to ever write my own eulogy, i think the words would spill out of my tongue like cursed poetry and stain the paper red.

Poem

Illicit

3. Illicit -//

how does it feel

for silence

to be the only language you're fluent in?

to live like the dead,

and to hear like the deaf?

how does it feel

for you to live only in hotel rooms

where the mirror

would never remember your face

hoping, almost believing,

that your reflections changed every time.

that no one knew who you are,

or who you had been.

for you to pretend

that the white linens

that smelled like shameless novelty

and shampoos that felt like bloodwater

were all you could take away?

how does it feel

for you to want someone so much

that you could set watersheds on fire.

like if you throw a penny into a wishing well,

you'll burn down the whole world

with wanting them.
for the insides of your blood to feel combustible?
how does it feel
to pierce your skin
with illicit apologies
during the times you couldn't align a smile? to feel so full of
yourself,
and yet all the more empty?

Poem

Summer

4. Summer -//

It's only after the last drop of rainfall
in a flood that you miss summer
and try
to swallow the water to save the world
until you realise the flood
was inside you
all along.
It's only when the canvas is finished
that the paint turns to blood
and my lungs spill themselves dry.
It's only when moments become memories that the echoes
turn into black pen scribbles
and I'm the torn paper
that feels every scratch.
Tell me, how do you ruin the ruination itself?

Poem

Dying Stars

5. Dying Stars -//

you told me i looked like your prayers
so i asked you
if you had ever begged to die.
You told me i looked like your prayers
so i asked you
if you had ever begged to die.
My body
spells out the word prey
far better
than my hands tear apart flesh.
i wonder if ill ever be able
to talk about the pain
without feeling it
all over again.
Something like
saying a name into the breeze
without hearing it echo back to me.
You will ask me about love
and i will tell you stories
about the aftermath
- heartbreak.
You will ask me about peace
and i will tell you about the cause

- wars.
You will ask me about truths
and i will tell you about the myths
because i am tired
of fighting this war
with the hope of
getting the peace i was never promised.
My hands ache
from the hope I've been holding on to;
my heart aches
from the love I've been trying to remember.
i adore the people who regret me;
i demolish the ones who glance at me.
You asked for my hand
and i gave you my body.
i have lived in this body my whole life
and she still treats me like a stranger;
a known stranger
who is growing more
and more
unfamiliar every day.
I am tired
of wanting the world so much
i am consumed by it;
tired
of wishing on stars
that are always dying.

Echoes of love in my throat
come out as screams of resentment
and it shatters the hope
bit by bit
everytime.
It's not the memories
we want to remember.
Its the love.
Always the love.

Poem

Would You Cry At My Funeral? Would You Even Attend?

6. Would You Cry At My Funeral? Would You Even Attend? -//

three,

when i heard the first fight,

five,

when i made lizard under the table my best friend.

seven,

when i grieved the death of my best friend all alone.

eleven,

when you first caught me seeking refuge under my bed.

"the noises are too loud" i said,

"please stop" i yelped.

constant whispers of doubting if i'm the reason

would it have been better without me?

am i the bandaid? am i the repellent?

you said i was your lizard best friend.

please love me enough to love each other;

please care for me enough to leave each other.

please keep her away from me

until you can keep her from yourself.

she isn't like this

you aren't like this
why am i turning out to be like that then?
a bad marriage
a broken house
me?
what made you this way
(this isn't you, i want to scream, but lizards can't speak)
how do i pick sides
if i want no part of this?
how i do distance myself
if this is all i've ever known?
how do i love now
without remembering the scars from before?
would you like me enough
to cry at my funeral?
would you stand each other enough
to even attend?
three,
when i heard the first fight.
all the years to follow,
i am the aftermath.

Abstract

Empty What-Ifs

7. Empty What-Ifs -//

I get it. You refreshing your feed every two seconds? I get it. Tick tock. Checking every app to see if anyone texted you? I get it You see, we are the same, you and i. Tick tock.

We tend to resort to things like these every time there's no one around, not because we are scared of feeling alone, feeling lonely, but because we are too scared of being overwhelmed. I get how it feels. Tick tock. To be overwhelmed by the little things that you notice only when you are all alone, with no one to distract you. With no one to tell you that you are going to get through this. With no one.

Little things, you ask? The ticking of the clock. The air that you breathe in. the air that leaves you. The empty what-ifs.

What if you are suddenly out of breath? What if you die right now, with no one around, and what if no one notices? Tick tock. What if you stare at the pointed knife too long, and what if it accidentally falls on you? What if in a few days your sweeper finally finds your dead body and then you become just another paragraph in a newspaper and the people you know cry about it for a day or two and then just... move on? Tick tock. Or worse, what if they don't have to move on because they were never really attached to you? Or even worse, what if they never move on?

What if in the after life you are just burdened with guilt about dying and leaving them all alone? What if there is no afterlife? Tick tock.

What happens then? I get that feeling. I get what it feels like to be alive only because you are afraid of the afterlife. I get what it feels like to want to embrace death because you're scared of life. I get it. Tick tock.

i hope you know you are not alone. i hope you know life wants to embrace you back. i hope.

Poem

Scattered Petals

8. Scattered Petals -//

..to be loved by her, its one of the most powerful things to be

:)

I know a girl

who loves so fiercely

so intensely

people almost start to fall in love with themselves.

I know a girl

who draws images

that run so close to the edge of the paper,

you can almost see them fall off

and you're scared

that they will either make you fall in love with them,

with her,

or you'll get eaten raw

by them,

by her.

I know a girl

who loves literature and flowers and Taylor Swift so much

she became a metaphor

for scattered petals

on a broken guitar string.

who is what Augustus is to a cigarette

that she is to the broken guitar

that she seldom wishes to get repaired
lying in the corner of her room
by the bookshelves.
I know a girl
who writes about pain
that one can never endure,
sings about loves
that were never meant to be,
and draws out secrets
that were never revealed
- simply because she knows me too,
or so i would like to think.
I know a girl
who laughs with the ones who wronged her
as she holds back curses
making songs
out of anguished screams
as if mercy came more naturally to her
than joy ever did.
I know a girl
and i can only hope
that she knows me too,
that she knows we see her.
That she taught us how to love
and we are glad
because it means we can give it back to her.
Maybe undressing God did harness art

for how else could you describe her;
the gift that never stops giving?

• 37 •

Poem

Love Them The Same

9. Love Them The Same -//

love them the same.
if only i could tell you about the little pieces of you that i find
in myself everyday
and the little fragments that i leave, hoping you find them in
yourself.
you and i are the same, you know
i do not know how to feel about that.
i do not know how to feel.
(please don't hate me)
"you're my daughter, we are the same"
fear consumes me as pride takes a walks along side
and i wish you could see that
i wish i could run to you and tell you all my problems and roll
your fingers in one by one as if 10 little problems is all i have
and then i realise that's exactly what i used to do with her back
then
and i stop.
i wish i could talk to you about my future without fearing i'll
turn into a replica of my past.
(i wish i could talk to her)
"you've your father's assertiveness"
should i be pleased? should i be watchful?

help, i want to scream
but alas, i have his pride too.
the one that walks with my mother's spitting image, but never
collides.
(i wish it did)
"your sister is just as empathetic"
how do i tell you
it's not empathy that runs in our veins
but fear
that you'll leave if we don't listen closely enough.
it's not just care
it's plotting our relationships with everyone exactly the way
we want to
because we have been at this for too long now,
too long,
and it hurts and i can't even tell you.
i can't tell you because i don't know how to.
how do i plot my own destruction?
(save me, please stay)
to be a person is to find pieces of yourself scattered in
everyone around you
and hope that they don't hate it as much as you do
to be a person is to hope that people will be able to love you
the same
to hope that you'll be able to love them the same.
(to be a person is to hope)

Poem

Autumn

10. Autumn -//

Love
is like iced tea
seeping through wooden floors.
cold, sweet, frozen.
Love
is a rancid fear
that has endured every toss and turn
of time,
and has wilted away
like the flowers at your grave.
There is a woman in my bathroom mirror
and I don't recognise
the scars on her cheeks.
She tells me
they're the birthmarks
of when God swallowed her whole
and she couldn't stop crying.
But then again,
she never did tell me
if she ever even believed in God.
My heart makes the same sound
as a tv static.
The elevators open

and I wait for the doors to close.
Just enough for love to escape/
/Just enough for me to be trapped.
Life is foreign and sticky
and love is familiar and something I can never really get hold
of.
But I'm not sure
if I even want to.
April radiates shadowy sepia luster
like your perfume
that sits on my table
on a warm day of autumn
as I read poems
about a dead woman's lover.
Understanding it a little too much
and feeling it a little too less.
The world relishes your shitty ultimatum, and the fog will
choke me up someday
and you'll be sorry.
But till then,
the woman in the window
will write poems and letters to the beyond
hoping they reach you.
She is new to this,
and she is starting to hate it already.
She doesn't know
what she hates more though -

being in love with a dead muse,
or
hoping.

Poem

Sunflower

11. Sunflower -//

Talking to you
feels like the happiness you get
when you're listening to a song
and you can tell
that the singer was smiling.
it feels
like that one intimate moment
between you and the book
you've just read the last words of
when you sit there
taking in the enormity of what you've just finished.
Only,
you know you create your own ending
Talking to you
feels like looking at the moon
for the first time,
every time.
or like the urge
to peel the moon
and separate it into two halves
and give one of them to you
because nothing else compares.

Abstract

Spring?

12. Spring? -//

"i am both, you know. i have been through both stages."

"what?"

"the things people call themselves. a hopeless romantic and a person who uses fear as a shield from love."

"what do you mean?" you say as you pick a flower and i call for more therapy.

"it has felt like a hunt to me. an eerie wail of something coming, hungry and knowing and longing." i have known longing more than i have known love, so much so that i fear I've confused the two.

you brush my hair back behind without my ear without thinking and I don't hold my breath anymore, not like i used to. you know i like it, and it makes me happy to see you do things because you know i like it.

"i don't know how to handle love when it is unveiled and vulnerable and delicate. and yet somehow fierce. i am used to love in a cacophony. sharp and angry. and ferocious."

"but?" you ask, almost hopeful. almost apologetic. for the hope, or for the assurance, i don't know.

"but despite all of myself, i find love again, and it finds me."

you smile at that, and i fall a little. just a little, like the flower you had in your hand that gently falls on the cushion as you play with my fingers. i have always loved it when you do that, and i like that you don't know that, because this way I know you're doing it because you love it too, because you feel like you have the right. its the little things, its mostly the little things about you.

you reach over a little more and squeeze my other hand while it lies on my shaking leg and I'm left with - is this love? not rushed like running, like escaping, but rather slow, like stretching.

like i know it won't be an escape from my problems, it would just make them easier because i know i have you. for whatever little time, but i do have you. like a garden party? like - oh, its spring, and i have remembered happy.

i want to tell you all of that. i always want to tell you every little thought that enters my mind, and often, i do. but this time, its different. not just because i am scared that the moment i say it out loud it will sound like a worded mirage and it will break the second air touches the insides of my tongue but because i want to hold on to this feeling a little longer, hold on to you a little longer i don't know how to hold love like a crown, like a flower. i don't know how to hold you. but if we get enough time, i will learn. i will understand.

and i know you already do. i can see it in the way you look at me just now, as if trying to tell me that well you know. that its our garden, and you will water the plants even on the days they have too many thorns. you caress the flower in your hand, and i squeeze a little tighter. right here, right now. enough, enough.

its a good thing you remind me of hope. its a good thing I've started to fall in love with hope. its a good thing. it doesn't matter if i start to long for you. this moment, right here, right now, i know that i have you with me. and that's enough. longing is okay, because i know that years from now, if i forget your face, i would still remember this moment. even if i forget your name, i would still remember that i had started to fall in love with you. i would remember you reminded me of hope. i would remember hope. i would remember.

Poem

To Love You In Memory

13. To Love You In Memory -//

i know love will hurt a little less this time,
even if it means
i have to burn in hell
just to be able to give you my warmth.
i know love has a middle name
that sounds just like your first name.
i know
that perhaps pink skies only exist
because i love you so deeply,
so much longer than i meant to,
that the earth felt it in its core.
i know
that every moment with you
will feel
like that one long hug
before the train leaves.
a sense of longing for you
while holding you still,
not wanting to let go,
while knowing deep down that i have to.
knowing
that i am happy loving you,

right now,
right here,
even if it means
i might have to let go.
i am happy
to have ever loved you,
to ever have been with you.
i will always
be happy to love you in memory,
even if the space i long for
no longer fits me.
i know
that i had fallen in love with hope,
and i fell in love with you right after,
and i think those are now synonymous.
hope for good things to continue.
i know that loving you will give me the strength to love the
world

Poem

Just Yours, Just Mine; Nothing's Ours

14. Just Yours, Just Mine; Nothing's Ours -//

if you were to break my heart again,

i hope you do it in a kinder way.

if you were to leave me now,

i hope you look back and smile.

just one last time.

if you were to stop loving me,

i hope you do it

with no guilt in your heart.

(please don't leave me)

if you were to keep loving me,

i hope you forget that the world will end.

if you were to look at me

i hope you get reminded of the little unicorn you had as a kid

the one you painted black because you thought it wouldn't

make it ugly

just unique, just yours.

if you were to hold me again,

i hope you remember the time you claimed to have touched

the rainbow because you ate an ice cream that had more than

three colours on it.

if you were to cry your heart out,

i hope you do it

wearing the sweater i gave you.
if you were to sing again,
i hope you find snippets of our jokes,
our conversations,
that revolved around
almost every song we heard.
i hope you never hate me enough to delete our playlists.
(please don't hate me.)
if you were to laugh again,
i hope you snort just like the old times
the times you said i'm the only one who can make you laugh
like that
and i hope, in some way, you remember me every time you
laugh.
it wouldn't be ugly
just unique, just mine.

Poem

What Memory Would You Want People To Remember You By?

15. What Memory Would You Want People To Remember You By? -//

i've been twelve and twitchy

thirteen and tensed

fourteen and forgettable

fifteen and faithless

sixteen and scarred

seventeen and stupid

eighteen and enraged.

i've been a mess

i've been the chaos

and i've been the volcano.

but

i've been twelve and thankful

thirteen and thoughtful

fourteen and forgiving

fifteen and fiery

sixteen and selfless

seventeen and soaring

eighteen and empathetic

i've been the peace

i've been the calm

i've been me.

what memory would i want people to remember me by, you ask?

maybe my handwriting

maybe the way i write the letter 's' with a different curl every time,

maybe the way i write with my hands slanted in a way that brings a chuckle on my old english teacher's face every time.

"it baffles me every time" she used to say.

it made me laugh every time, i think.

or maybe it is the way i speak

the way i answer every call with a sappy "hellooo" that makes others laugh,

the way i blurt out words and start stammering and then chide myself for thinking too fast,

the way i make a clicking sound with my tongue every time i say a word with repeated letters.

or or

maybe it is the way i write as if i am talking to the person in real time

the way i text as if i am holding hands with the other person

greet as if i hope i actually mean something to someone.

or maybe it is the way i love

the way i will order your favourite food for myself on days i miss you the most,

the way i would leave notes for you to read

hoping that someday you feel the same way,

the way i would tell you about the time i used to call my
favourite chocolate with a different name as a kid
or when Maa used to turn on the radio
when i was a few months
and i would talk gibberish as if the noises on the radio were
trying to converse with me.
maybe it is the way i'm slowly learning to love myself
maybe it is the way my words make you feel
maybe it is the way i hope that my art is worth something to
you
(please don't forget me. please remember me.)

A Note Of Thanks

Thank You for reading this book; it truly means the world to me.

For any reviews, suggestions or constructive criticism, please write an email to sukritisinha@gmail.com or send a text to @sukritiiiii_ on Instagram!